Insect World

Butterflies

by Mari Schuh

Bullfrog Books

Ideas for Parents and Teachers

Bullfrog Books let children practice nonfiction reading at the earliest reading levels. Repetition, familiar words, and photo labels support early readers.

Before Reading

- Discuss the cover photo. What does it tell them?
- Look at the picture glossary together. Read and discuss the words.

Read the Book

- "Walk" through the book and look at the photos. Let the child ask questions. Point out the photo labels.
- Read the book to the child, or have him or her read independently.

After Reading

- Prompt the child to think more. Ask: Have you ever seen a butterfly? Where was it flying? What color was it?

The author dedicates this book to Caroline Noonan of Racine, Wisconsin.

Bullfrog Books are published by Jump!
5357 Penn Avenue South
Minneapolis, MN 55419
www.jumplibrary.com

Library of Congress Cataloging-in-Publication Data
Schuh, Mari C., 1975-
Butterflies / by Mari Schuh.
p. cm. -- (Insect world)
Summary: "This photo-illustrated book for early readers tells how butterflies find food and briefly explains their life cycle. Includes picture glossary"--Provided by publisher.
ISBN 978-1-62031-053-3 (hardcover : alk. paper) -- ISBN 1-62031-053-8 (hardcover : alk. paper) -- ISBN 978-1-62496-045-1 (ebook) -- ISBN 1-62496-045-6 (ebook)
1. Butterflies--Juvenile literature. 2. Butterflies--Food--Juvenile literature. 3. Butterflies--Life cycles--Juvenile literature. I. Title. II. Series: Schuh, Mari C., 1975- Insect world.
QL544.2.S3883 2014
595.78'9--dc23   2012039938

Series Editor   Rebecca Glaser
Book Designer   Ellen Huber
Photo Researcher   Heather Dreisbach

Photo Credits: Alamy, 16tl, 23bl; Dreamstime, 3t, 10–11, 24; Getty, 7, 17; iStock, 1, 6, 18, 23tr; Stutterstock, cover, 3b, 4–5, 8–9, 13-14, 16bl, 20–21, 22, 23br; SuperStock, 12, Veer, 15, 19, 23tl

Printed in the United States of America at Corporate Graphics in North Mankato, Minnesota.
4-2013 / P.O. 1003

10 9 8 7 6 5 4 3 2 1

Table of Contents

Lots of Butterflies

It's a sunny day. Butterflies fly in the garden.

They look for food.

5

Where will they find it?

Let's see!

antenna

Thin antennas smell.

Here is the food.

Sip. Sip.
See its long
tongue?

tongue

10

It sips nectar.

Zoom! Zoom!

scales

They fly and fly.
They use their
four wings.
Tiny scales give
the wings color.

**Butterflies taste flowers.
They use their feet.
They find the best ones.**

They lay eggs.

15

Caterpillars hatch.

They eat and eat.
They grow.

pupa

The caterpillar
forms a shell.

Now it is a pupa.

The pupa changes.

Now it is a butterfly.

It looks for food.
Fly, butterfly, fly!

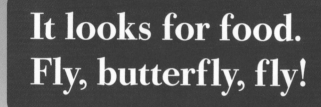

21

Parts of a Butterfly

antenna
A thin feeler on a butterfly's head that it uses to smell and feel.

eyes
A butterfly has two big eyes to help it see in many directions.

wings
A butterfly has four wings. Butterfly wings are often bright colors.

tongue
A butterfly's long tongue curls up when it's not in use.

legs
A butterfly has six legs, like all insects.

Picture Glossary

caterpillar
The wormlike creature that later changes into a butterfly.

pupa
The third stage of a caterpillar's life; pupas change into butterflies.

hatch
To break out of an egg.

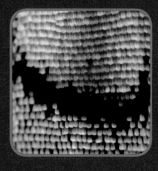

scales
Tiny, thin parts that cover a butterfly's wings, body, and legs.

Index

To Learn More

Learning more is as easy as 1, 2, 3.

1) Go to www.factsurfer.com

2) Enter "butterfly" into the search box.

3) Click the "Surf" button to see a list of websites.

With factsurfer.com, finding more information is just a click away.